Old Loves Are Seldom Finished ... When New Loves Begin

bj King

Old Loves Are Seldom Finished ... When New Loves Begin

bj King

Copyright © 2025 by bj King

Published by 1st World Publishing
P.O. Box 2211, Fairfield, Iowa 52556
tel: 641-209-5000 • fax: 866-440-5234
web: www.1stworldpublishing.com

First Edition

ISBN Softcover: 978-1-4218-3590-7

LCCN: Library of Congress Cataloging-in-Publication Data

All rights reserved. No part of this book may be reproduced or utilized in any form or by any means, electronic or mechanical, including photocopying or recording, or by any information storage and retrieval system, without permission in writing from the author.

This material has been written and published for educational purposes to enhance one's well-being. In regard to health issues, the information is not intended as a substitute for appropriate care and advice from health professionals, nor does it equate to the assumption of medical or any other form of liability on the part of the publisher or author. The publisher and author shall have neither liability nor responsibility to any person or entity with respect to loss, damages, or injury claimed to be caused directly or indirectly by any information in this book.

I dedicate this book to the men who came for blessing.

Introduction

The Muse within me
Desires expression
She's spoken 'naught before
For she's needed inspiration
Not found in blood or gore
The muse is out now
Filling pages with words of love
Maybe no one else will read
Or maybe they will
And share a tear
Or a chuckle
If they can see themselves
In the some of me
I've written on these pages
For all the World to see.

Edward

In '76 I was 35 and in a rut
Doing everything for everyone to prove I was O.K.
Taking valium by the handful
To ease the pains of doubt.
A new priest came to our church.
He said, "You are O.K."
"God loves you."
But he expected much of me
I bake-saled, committeed,
And worked harder
To prove to him I was O.K.
He confronted us all with Jesus,
How He had lived and how He had died,
And what that meant.
He offered us a chance for a personal relationship
With our God.
Many were afraid and ran away.
Some stayed to verbally crucify him for
His suggestion of a personal religion.
They loved their impersonal church,
Their safe brand of religion.
He threatened change,
They had their private meetings,
Planned how to "handle" him,
This outsider who was "ruining" their church
They played games, mind games.
He paid, his family paid.
I stayed by their side
And listened and prayed and watched.
Three years past.
I watched this vibrant man of God grow tired

From abuse and frustration,
Forget how to smile,
Forget how to laugh,
Inhibit his capacity to love.
Many parishioners moved to other churches
Or had "life changing" experiences
And stayed to reap the benefits.
When things were smooth again
He took a look at himself
This man of God.
He was tired, energy spent,
Creativity exhausted,
He had to get away.
He talked to God.
God said, "Thanks, My Son, for a job well done"
"It's time for you to move on."
So he did.
He took his family to Oklahoma
To start anew,
Yet in an old capacity for him.
He had been in geology before.
God opened some doors
And he fit right in again
But his heart still ached
For someone to share his dream.
Someone to love him,
To accept him totally.
My Mother died the day he left our town
And so did a part of me.
He wrote to me to let me know he cared,
That God cared.
I answered and let him know I cared.
Now that he was gone
I felt safe to let him know I cared.
My caring sparked a flame in him long dead.
He wrote to me and I answered

We poured out our hearts,
Our hurts, our pasts,
Our hopes, our dreams,
And fell deeper in love.
I was scared,
I was married,
So was he.
What should we do?
Give up, Give in?
Stay in our ruts?
"They" said I shouldn't,
"They" said I couldn't,
It was not "right",
I pondered
I labored
And I cried.
"They" couldn't
"They" shouldn't
But I could
And I would
Take a chance
To finally be happy.
Freedom is expensive,
It can cost you
Money
Family
Friends
Position
I said "Goodbye"
To the house
We had spent endless hours searching for
Hours rebuilding to suit our needs
Our personalities.
"Goodbye" to the sunroom
We had built together,
"Goodbye" to hours spent in solitude there

Discovering my "real" self.
I found
I could no longer stay in "our" house
Without our love.
It had become a mortgage payment
A drudgery to clean
Something to insure
That I could no longer
Emotionally afford.
"Goodbye" to a garage
That I could never keep clean
A yard I could never keep mowed
"Goodbye" to our pretty yellow bedroom
Which we so seldom shared.
"Goodbye" to the basement
Where we were supposed
To feel safe from storms.
"Goodbye" to the sewing room
Which changed from cozy to claustrophobic
After mother's death.
"Goodbye" to the kitchen
Where I'd baked a million cookies
And read a thousand books.
"Goodbye" to an attic full of memories.
"Goodbye" to a den too dark to read in-
Which was my passion
But perfect for watching TV-
His passion
"Goodbye" to happy times
In front of the fireplace.
I had to say "Goodbye".
Freedom can cost you
Your place in life
But it can give you more-
Yourself
Peace

A new place in life
Less need for money
New friends
And peace.
Edward left his family and started back to school.
His creativity returned.
His manhood returned.
His zest for living returned.
My children and I followed
Edward to Oklahoma.
He was my pillow and my blanket
As my legs entwined with his
I felt his warmth
Not just of his body
But of his soul.
He helped me to make me whole
Reaching out to him as I slept
I was reaching within myself
When we were awake again
I spoke to him
And for the first time in months
I heard myself.
I spoke the truth
Maybe not the truth
For Tom or Dick or Jane
But my truth
And maybe yours.
The truth we have to learn to live with
Grow with
The truth we must learn to believe.
A resurrection of faith
Faith lost in time and space
Crowded out by people
And bodies
And noise.
Faith I had drowned

Repeatedly in pills and gin.
Faith in myself
Faith I found reflected
In his eyes
His smile
His touch
Faith I heard myself
Explain to him
Until I could feel myself
Feeling it again
Faith resurrected in myself
In him
And in my God.
Thank God.
For four days we lived together
Ate together
Laughed together
Wept together
Prayed together
Walked together
Loved together
We were finally content.
Death came for him that night.
I watched the pain contort his face and body.
I held him.
I screamed.
I cried.
I breathed for him,
Until the ambulance came.
But he was dead
I cried for him
For me, for us,
For my children,
For his children,
For his wife of eighteen years,
Who could not understand

Why we had to be together.
I still cry often
But I am glad I came.
I'm glad I loved him
And he loved me.
I feel it was meant to be.
My children went back to Texas.
Their Father came for them.
He was so kind, so caring
We were free to come "home" again
But I could not go back.
I had to go forward
So I walked
I rocked
I read
I cried and
I prayed.
"They" say I built you
Into more than what you were-
A man
"They" say you had become my God.
How odd
That "They" could know so much more than I
What you were to me.
You set me free
You let me be
You did not question, "Why?"
But looked me in the eye
And said "I love you, I care",
How rare.
We touched
And then we parted
The choice was not our own.
I wish I could call
You on the phone
Just to hear your voice.

I would still make the choice.
Love is the only answer I have
To all the "Whys?"
I spent the next months
Rocking
Reading
Reaching inside myself
For some answers to the "Whys?"
I tried to get some grasp on
Tried to get a clear image of
Who am I?
Who am I really?
All of my roles were removed
Was there a "me" without the roles?
Death removed my role as daughter
Divorce removed my role as John's wife
Distance removed the children
So I was a mother in name only
At a distance I could not accept as functional
The Episcopal Church removed the sacraments
And my role as a church leader
My father remarried immediately
And no longer needed me.
Death removed Edward.
He had seemed my one sure reason for being
But he is gone and yet "I AM"
Who am I?
What does God want me to do?
How does it happen?
That I am in this place
On this planet
At this time?
The ring of the phone reminds me
My role of friend has not been removed
Before and after all else
We are called

"To love one another".
In the midst of the depression
I am still grateful
That I came, that I am in this place
With God's trees, rocks, hills,
Birds, squirrels, possums,
Sunrises and sunsets,
And today the rain.
For here I will be able to endure
To start over, to rebuild
To find a new direction.
Several months ago
When I was trying to decide to leave Lubbock
The therapist asked
"What is the worst thing that could happen?"
My reply was
"For Ed to encourage me to come to Oklahoma
And then desert me, or leave me there alone"
Is God telling me that in my worst fears
He is with me?
That even if the worst things I can imagine happen
That if I have faith He is still there
To help me?
I think so.
The peace I feel
When I have every reason to feel panic
Has to be a gift of the Spirit
I awoke at dawn and felt the need to see the sunrise
It is not as spectacular as some I've seen
But to me it is spectacular in that it does
Still rise and set.
In spite of all else that goes on in this World is that the one remaining certainty?

Mother Love

You've gone now from your body
But I feel you still
I hear you still
When I wake up at night
And wonder, "What would Mother think or do?
You're with me there
In spirit
'Though your mortal form's deceased
I hear you clearly on some evenings
As you talk to me
Through lectures long remembered
From sitting at your knee
You sense now when I need your presence
And you still come to me
For dying doesn't stop the sharing
Of a Mother's love

Christmas

Christmas is strange this year
I am a visitor in my home
Because I chose to move away
To make a new life
The children are here
There is love
But it seems over-shadowed by
Remote-control cars and stereos.
My son, who is six, does not understand
We are celebrating the birth of Christ
Why should he?
I am too confused and pained to try to explain to him
He knows all about Santa Claus
 And the names of all the reindeer.
I don't feel strong enough
To fight the commercialization of Christmas
In my pain I get caught up in the buying myself.
Somehow there must be a way
To let them know I care, God cares
This is not the way.
Christmas is very different this year.
My mother is dead.
Her home is still there
Her tree was erected
But there was no
"Handmade with love from Grandma"
Any where about.
The stockings were hung
On her chimney, but not filled,
Because my Mother is dead.
And another woman

Tries her best to be "Grandma"
But forgets to fill the stockings she's hung,
So it's not the same,
Mom did it with love all year.
There are just some things
Which cannot be bought, reproduced, or replaced
We should not try.
Life must go on,
I forget just why.
Her grave has a new expensive marker
For everyone to see
My heart aches because
Nothing can be done
To change a thing
To make it hurt less.
We must endure.
I forget just why.
My chest aches,
Because nothing can be said
Nothing can be done
To change a thing
To make it hurt less.
It seems the name of the game of life
Is endurance.
Christmas is strange this year
The love I left my family for is dead.
Our plans for an untinseled meaningful Christmas
Died with him.
Here I sit amidst the chaos of paper,
Ribbons, batteries and noise,
And weep for "what might have been".
How will I survive?
Without my best friend?
Without my family?
I was finally free with Edward.
Free to tell him everything

About my judgments and values,
To expose my fears and frustrations
To admit my failures and shame,
To share my triumphs.
With him I learned who I can become
And now he's dead.
Can there ever be anyone else
To share everything with?
It seems so impossible
And is it worth the pain?
The pain of loss from having so much
Invested in loving another Human being?
God, it hurts!
There is a huge vacant place in my middle,
Such tightness in my chest
The only relief seems to be in tears,
Racking sobs
And they come totally unannounced,
Triggered by something as small as a yellow rose
Or as vivid as watching another heart attack victim
In a movie.
I am relieved that I can
Usually give in to the tears,
Lean into the pain
For a few moments of relief.
After each episode of tears
I wonder.
They say, "Time will heal".
Does that mean I have to give up my good memories,
To quit hurting?
I choose to remember
The months of correspondence
The four days of our life together.
It was too "good", too "real"
To be blocked out the way I did so many
Memories before.

Edward had helped me
By holding my hand across the miles
As I spent the summer writing out
So many of my blocked out memories,
And encouraging me to face myself
Without the Valium.
We wanted to find a way, a place
To live the better life, the reflected life
With more meaning, more feeling
Than the drug-filled life I had existed in
For the past fifteen years.
I cannot give up
I have come too far
Out of the darkness to allow myself to sink
Back into oblivion
Just for security.
This was not the time to begin blocking out again
But the old tapes were there
Still in my head
"Just forget about it"
"Push it into your sub-conscious"
"You don't have to remember"
"It's too painful".
But the reality is
Even if we choose not to remember
It all still has to be dealt with sometime
"But I can't deal with this alone, Lord!" I cried.

May Rainbows Be About You

It does not feel as if it is my last day to live.
Does one really feel the end drawing close?
Did Edward know?
Does that explain his insistence to go against convention?
We were both such moral and conventional people.
I guess I will never know.
As I watch the sunrise
I hear a crow, an alarm clock, a door slamming,
A baby crying and a small bird tweeting.
There are days when I know how the small bird feels
But God gave him the power to fly.
Facing surgery tomorrow in an unknown hospital is scary,
But the lumps in my breasts will not wait.
I bought a book of poetry entitled
<u>May Rainbows Be About You</u>
The clerk said, "The author lives here"
"Would you like to meet him?"
I said, "I would, I need someone to talk to."
She gave him my number
And he called
He said, "May rainbows be about you".
I said, "You're crazy".
He replied, "Come to tea and see".
I did, he held my hand and listened.
He held my heart and cared.
He held me and we shared.
He held my hand before and after surgery.
I did not want to face the surgery without communion
 And because of another wonderful priest
Who visited us in the hospital
And not only listened to our stories

But "heard" us
We three shared
One of the most meaningful communions of our lives.
In the weeks that followed
We laughed, we cried, we fought,
We ran, we played, and we fought.
We loved and we prayed.

Lou

I grew to love the crazy poet from Newfoundland
And he learned to love and cherish me
"The crazy lady from Texas".
We are so different.
Our pasts could not meet,
But we understood each other's childhood pain.
Our futures were as unrehearsed as running in the rain
And yet we loved each other,
Of this there was no doubt.
Why had God let our paths cross in Edmond, Oklahoma?
"Why, God?" I shout.
God says, "Why not? You need each other and I will help".
Because I remain off the Valium,
I cannot understand why he starts to drink again
After five years of sobriety.
He tells me that he's dying
I watch him bear the pain
God gives us strength.
My son comes to live with me.
God gives the poet love to replace the jealousy
It's hard for him to watch me love my son
When his own mother left so much for him undone.
We travel, we share, we care.
I cry, "God, why me?"
God says, "Wait in love and see".
We sit in a bar in Santa Fe
And I write poetry for him.

If I agree to love you
If I agree to hold your hand
If I agree to sit with you and

Speak of things I've never shared
Can I trust you?
Trust you to love me
Trust you to reach out your hand
Trust you to walk with me
Places you would rather not go
Trust you to sit with me and
Listen and not judge
But share your secrets too
Can I trust you?
If I agree to love you
Can you trust me?
So many questions
So few answers
Our lives are filled with "ifs" and "if onlys"
If only we had met when we were younger
If only we had more time
If only we had more money
If only our families had been different
If only our families were different now
If the whole world were different
We would still have only us and
What we decide will still be up to us
Because God gave us Freewill
We can ponder all the "ifs" and
Enumerate all the "if onlys" and
Waste our today dreading or
Looking forward to tomorrow
But, my friend, all we have is today
And if we waste that we are fools and
All the "if onlys" in the World can't change that
So we traveled on
And laughed
And cried
And prayed
And wrote more songs along the way

Will you sit awhile with me?
We can share some time and tea
Will you let me hold your hand?
I will try to understand
Would you? Could you? Should you?
Will you let me hold your heart?
Please don't let it fall apart
Will you give yourself a chance?
Will you choose to take a stance?
Would you? Could you? Should you?
Will you let yourself trust me?
And in doing so be free
Can you face life without a plan?
Reach out now and take my hand
Would you? Could you? Should you?
Will you take a chance with me?
To share love, it's free
Dare you let me come inside?
Where alone you do abide
Would you? Could you? Should you?
Will you walk with me a while?
Feel your soul is not on trial
Can you accept things as they are?
Not looking back or ahead too far?
Would you? Could you? Should you?
Will you hold me in your arms?
Where I feel safe from all life's harms
There we can touch each other's hearts
Until it's time for us to part
Would you? Could you? Should you?
Will you share some life with me?
For all the World to see
Do you dare to take a chance?
So we can share in life's romance
Would you? Could you? Should you?
We've every reason to run away

We've been hurt, we've had to pay
But I believe God has a plan
We do not have to understand.
Because with faith I still have hope
We will, we can, we should -- reach out.
I love you, I love you, I love you.
I do, it's true
So hard for me to say
So easy for me to do
I once tried to love a boy with a crew cut
I could not do it right
He preferred boys
I once tried to love a salesman,
Security, prestige.
I could not do it right
I did once love a man of God, a priest
Very much a man, yet a boy with me
But he died, and I cried
Then I reached out to love again
And God sent a poet, a Yankee
And I said, "I cannot love this man, Lord"
"It's too hard, send someone else"
But I reached out in love and
He sent me strength
To love and care about this man of God, a poet
And -- we did it right, he and God and I

The poet tells me I'm lovely
Even though I have my glasses on
He tells me that I'm beautiful
Even when my hair is wet
He tells me that he loves me
Isn't that amazing?
I thought I had to have every hair in place
Put my best foot forward
Have my contacts in

Before I could be lovable
Isn't it amazing?
I love him
When he has his glasses on
With his beard and mustache
With his teeth in or out
Even when I'm taller than he is
Isn't that amazing?
Love is beautiful
But love is not blind
Love accepts it all
Just as it is
And doesn't ask for more
Be yourself
Give it a try
The lovable you comes from inside

Don't be afraid to love me
I will help you die
But first I will help you live
You can take my hand and laugh
You can take my hand and cry
Try to love
Try to be free
Try to know God
Try to live before we die
Together we will try
You climbed a mountain in Santa Rosa, My Love
We watched the sunset in Las Vegas
We made love in Santa Fe
And several places along the way
In Taos the moon came up
Just as the sun went down
We marveled at God's creation once again
We laughed and loved
And then we cried again

How does life keep getting better in New Mexico?
I'm not sure
Maybe it's because God's with us
This we know for sure
Every chapel has His feeling
Every mountain shows His strength
Why are you to endure the pain, my love
I have no idea
But I know I was to be here with you
Not to ease the pain; I can't
But to hold you as you endure
Albuquerque does not rhyme, you are right
But Spirit is here in the faces of the people
In the plaza as we play and dance
The lilac that you borrowed just for us
The scent brings back my childhood
And even that is good
Spirit has been with us
We have experienced so many new things together
And they are good and beautiful and right
What comes next?
We do not know
But our togetherness eases our fears
And makes us able to look ahead
Instead of looking back
And this too is very good
For people such as us
Who have felt the pain
And know the price is high
But worth the cost
You traded beer and shots
For margaritas and champagne
With your lady
You traded fear and tears
For laughter and love
With your lady

There is still the pain
Time and time again
Spirit was with you on the mountain
He was with you by the streams
He was with you in my arms
He was with you in the chapels
But no more than in my bed as you cried
"Oh, God!" and I answered
"Thank God!"
He loves us everywhere
We are his children
The alcohol took the poet from me
And again I was left alone

My Daughter

Into the phone I ask
"When are you coming?"
Her period of silence
Says more than any words
Her answer, without being verbalized is
"I don't want to come at all, I'm too busy."
She verbalizes what
She thinks I want to hear
"We will be there Sunday."
"But," defensively she adds.
"I want to be back home for my birthday."
They are not questions so much
As challenges she throws
Her statements hit me in the gut
Ander rises from there to my head
Logic and reason leave
Anger reigns again
Rejection in red neon letters
Fills my being
The pain engulfs me
I try desperately to remain calm
Desperate not to cry
Not to let her know
The power I give her to hurt me
Loving her is difficult
Not loving her is impossible
She is my child
She is me
At twelve she is me at sixteen
As I hang up the receiver
I collapse in tears

Pounding the counter
In frustration
Why did I call?
Why didn't I wait?
Why do I put myself through this?
I speak to her father later by phone
He understands my pain
He had known her wishes
But could not bear to deliver the message
We are caught again
In a dilemma of our own making
A "no win" situation
We vow to once again
Cause as little pain as possible
I agree to let her have her wish
But refuse to invite her again
Until she "asks" to come
Fearing that she will not ask
Can I live with my decision?
Even as I hang up the phone
I am reaching for a pad and pen
To say, "I love you"
You are welcome in my day"
"I understand"
"I am here and I am with you"
Somehow as I put it all on paper
Some of my anger leaves
I am made aware
She is "being"
She is doing
Her own thing
The "right" I am fighting for
For myself
I also defend for her
Even though the pain engulfs me
She is the one I wanted to be

The one with enough will to rebel
No "yes person" she
Again I scream
"God, why me?"
And even as I utter the sounds
I'm chuckling
"Because you dared to risk"
"You dared to care"
"And you still do"
"And you still will"
"Even though to do so causes pain"
"You will again and again"
"Because you are my child and I love you."

Old Loves Are Seldom Finished When New Loves Begin

Here I sit on my bed alone
The evening was filled with
Drinks
Music
Laughter
Theirs, not mine
I was inside myself watching me
Watching them
And wondering, why?
Here I sit on my bed alone
Alone and lonely
But less is the pain
Of being alone
When the alternative is
Being with just anyone
What I seek
Seems to be a missing link
To another World
One I've lost sight of
A World where we loved
And played
And laughed
And believed in love
Spring is here
But there is still the fear
The air feels and smells the same
As it did then
The redbud and the lilac bloom
Maybe it's too soon to fall in love again
But the World is not such a pleasant place to be

Without someone to hold
To be held by
Someone to care for
To hope with
To weep with
To laugh with
The World is not a pleasant place to be
If we try to fill the void with many people
Noise and restless activity
Because there is still the void
So I returned once more to the church
I found a group of single people
All suffering varied degrees of pain
As singles
We observe others closely
We judge
We question
We compare
And occasionally
We reach out
We share
A joke
A drink
Our beds
Our bodies
And occasionally
We reach out
We hide ourselves
In movies
In booze
In bed
In books
In television
In work
In sports
In music

In dance
And yet occasionally
We reach out
We have been
Lied to
Used
Abused
Loved, abandoned
Loved, criticized
Loved, possessed
Loved, rejected
Yet occasionally
We still reach out
We have trouble
Being alone
Being in crowds
Being in pairs
Being ourselves
Being honest
Being trusting
And yet occasionally
We still reach out
We want
To feel loved
To feel accepted
We want
No complications
No commitments
No one to tell us what to do
Or how to live our lives
We want to be free
So occasionally we still
Reach out
What we find out there are others like ourselves
Afraid to trust
Afraid to love

Afraid to reach out
We've every reason to run away
We've been hurt
We've had to pay
But I believe God has a plan
We do not have to understand
Because with faith, I still have hope
We will
We can
We should
Reach out and I did
I went back to work
And I met a man
A banker, he was running
Even harder than I
I tried to reach out to him
It pains me, my friend, to watch you run away
From life
From me
From love
From happiness
From peace
And yet I understand
Your running
From more pain
From commitment
From responsibility
From trouble
From me
We both have our pasts
To contend with
To pay for
To repent
To forgive
To run away from
I'm not sure what I expect from you

Tenderness
Honesty
Caring
Consideration
Do I expect too much?
I cannot promise you
Forever
No pain
No complications
No disagreements
But I do offer you
Love
Consideration
Honesty
Tenderness
Compassion
Friendship
Physical comfort and
Moral support
I see you with your back to the wall
Confusion creeping in
Trust receding
Bitterness apparent
Feel your tension seeking escape
When I hold you I feel
Your tension ease
You trust me
You stop running
When you hold me I feel
Safe
Sure
Calm
Relaxed
Protected from the World
The things we do not say
Make me doubt

Make me uncomfortable
Distrustful
Tense
When we talk I feel
Calmer
More confident
More sure of who you are
More sure of who I am
I'm still not sure of why we've met
Or where our lives will go from here
I only know I care about you
I have taken you into my life and
I cannot run or walk away
He could
And he did
With someone seventeen years younger
Whom he felt could offer him
Forever
No pain no complications
No disagreements
He lives in another city now
And we talk by phone occasionally
They fight constantly
He is ill most of the time
He's changing jobs again
And I'm grateful we are still friends
Because
Old loves are seldom finished
When new loves begin
We can love a dozen people
And still not have a friend
Friendship's more important
And needs to be retained
When the fires of passion
We choose not to light again
Some people touch our lives and leave scars

Some people pass through our lives and leave nothing
Some people help us heal the scars others have left
A lifetime of loneliness
I cannot face
But a day alone
I can enjoy
I've learned that married
Isn't necessarily better
For all it's wonderful intimacy
Where two people can share more
With a private joke
Or a significant look
Than most people
With a thousand words
I've learned that single
Isn't necessarily better
For all it's freedom to be
I've learned that now is better
For it's my chance to be alive
To grow

My Friend

My friend, I love you
I've watched you walk through hell
Hell of rejection
Hell of abandonment
Hell of loss of those you've loved
Your pain is very real
My pain in sharing with you is real
I feel so helpless
I feel so angry
How can I make you see?
How unique you are
Fear has caused tenseness
To replace calm
Restless activity to replace
Deliberate actions
Your friendly open smile
To become a hesitant look
You verbally negate
Things I know you believe in
You try to convince me
How much fun you have
Getting drunk
How much safer to love a married man
How much easier life is
Without the complications of attachments
At times you seem to hate me
Because I won't give up
Won't hate men with you
I can't
They are people just like you and me
With needs and parents

Ex-wives and children
Just like you and me
They've been rejected
And lied to
And taken advantage of
Just like you and me
In your head you seem to have
Him all arranged
Acceptable profession
Acceptable build
Acceptable lack of children
Acceptable manners
Acceptable age
Until all your stipulations are met
You will save your love
Saving love, to me
Is like saving rain water
It evaporates
And the container cracks
And becomes brittle and hard
You cannot accept
That I can love more
Than one man
Are you judging me?
Or are you judging you?
You say, "But I'm not like you"
"I can't be that way"
I'm not asking you to be like me
And neither should you
You are not me
And I am not you
You are unique
I am unique
Our basic needs are the same
To be loved
To be cared for

To have someone to share with
I understand your reluctance
But I have to reach out to you
I love you
And I care

Self Discovery

As I discover myself
I learn
I am one of many
A symbol
Understanding more
Women of yesterday and today
The mute ones of the past
The inarticulate
Who took refuge behind men
Behind children
And many behind wordless institutions
The women of today
All action and knowing
Running, becoming copies of men
As I search within
I find a "me" that is
Somehow in between
I yearn to fly back to my children
On wings I do not possess
To hide behind their needs
And make them my own
I vacillate between finding
A man to take care of me
And finding a man to take care of
The 'real' me fights to balance
Between action and contemplation
Involvement and self preservation
Emotion and intellect
Depression occurs when
I despair of ever reconciling
These warring elements

Despair comes when I try to find
A universal meaning to my entire life
It feels absurd, illogical
Void of meaning, without purpose
I lose perspective and become depressed
I want to retreat from life and people
I must find a retreat for my fragmented self
Happiness with Human beings
Is so precarious
Some can allow you to love them
Or think they can
Yet when they discover you really do
They run away feeling
Threatened undeserving
Others can love you
Even though you are illusive, detached
And unable to give your full self to them
Some just want to run and play
Which would be fine
Except they're married
When in Canadian county
Or at least their wives are
Others declare
"I will love you, and you can be you"
But when that "you"
Does not conform to their needs
Or you cannot be found
The words lose all meaning
And become yet another lie
I resent men who are afraid
Of a women's strength
I am not loud, aggressive,
Demanding of my rights
I am soft, indirect
Delicate, tender, feminine
But I contain strength

Just the same
Maybe this type of strength
Is even harder for a man
To combat or accept
Than the aggressive vocal
Competitive feminism
I refuse to become political
To fight for causes
Politics touch me
In terms of taxes and freedoms
I can pay more taxes
And drive on poorer streets
I can watch my children be bused
And hate it
But not fight back
What will it take to make
Me angry enough to act?
My pattern has been not to act
To run away
Avoid the person
Avoid the scene
I turn away inside myself
Live mostly in my own World
Without TV
The newspaper
And the TV news
I cannot divide life
Into political parties
And teams
Perhaps my problem has been
I expect my dreams
My plans, my wishes to happen
A wish for me is not a dream
But a creation
If I can see something
In my mind

I feel I should be able to create it
To make it happen
Perhaps this is not possible
Maybe this is not even sane
The World is filled with other people
Dreaming dreams they never expect to happen
Allowing myself to become
A part of someone else's dream
To share a dream
But no understanding of reality
Causes pain
When dream eventually confronts reality
And I am ready to get on with the dream
Which for me means making the dream
Become reality
The other person is aghast
"Did you really believe all that?"
"You are really naive!"
I guess I am
When I enter a room full of people
I feel anxiety
I cannot be with cynics, callous,
Hard-boiled, superficial people
I see below the surface
Sometimes I hate it
There is no way back
To the other way of life
I want to run far away
To get away from the "self"
But I am learning
The "self" is my shadow
It will follow me anywhere I go
I must confront it
We must do battle
I must conquer
My self, my guilt

At this time I must live very fast
Place many people
Between me and my past
Because it is still a burden
A ghost
When I try to write the interior
Constant dialogue
That occurs in my head
It is difficult
There is no punctuation
No spelling
It flows
Like a river
Invading my sleep
My work, my play
Distracting me from people
Making concentration on daily routine
Almost impossible
Oh, Lord, show me the way
What price must I pay?
You show me a way in and out of the pain
Over and over again
Show me who to love
Which resentments to rise above
How to still my shaking
In the dilemma of my own making
Which way shall I go?
Will I ever know?
Will the answers ever come?
God, I feel so dumb!
You have given me the intellect
And I have become suspect
Of everyone you send
Is this on a true friend?
Will this one love me and leave?
Then again I will grieve

I cry out again each day
Lord, show me the way
His answer comes again
"Give your love freely
But retain your 'self'
For when the ones you love have gone
For whatever reason
You will desperately need your 'self'"

Child Remembered

I went back to a therapist to find
How I got to be me
He invited me again into my past
Go back in time to three or four
Can you walk through a door
And remember when
How did you feel then?
Was it anger you felt?
Did she hit you with a belt?
No, just her hand
Did you take a stand?
No, she was bigger than I
All I did was cry
And wish I could be good
Good enough so I could
Do all the things that mommies do
Like cook and sew and plan
I'm angry with me
'Cause I'm only three
And I'm angry with her
Because she won't let me stir
She says I'm too small
And that's not all
She says I have to learn
First before I can
Use her pots and pans
Or her sewing machine
My hands might not be clean
Oh, she's so mean!
She makes me mad!
But when I talk back she's sad

And she calls me "bad"
How come she hits my dad?
And he hits her back
Because they have a pact
It's all right for them
To get mad
"Cause they're grown up
When you are small
And you are not very tall
Big people can make you feel
Like you're not very real
Just 'cause you aren't grown yet
Doesn't make you a pet
Kids have feelings too
Just like me and you
Lots of time they feel scared
That's a feeling that I've shared
When I was small
It was not much fun at all
No one seemed to try to understand
They just raised their hand
And told me what to do
I don't think it's right, do you?
Now that I'm grownup
I guess I am fed up
With being told what
I can't do
I know it isn't true
I have my freedom now
Yet I still wonder
How can I feel so scared
When I'm all grown up?
Must I go back to when
I was maybe ten
Or further back
To find out what I lack

What causes me to be unhappy with me?
I'm lying here in bed
With anger in my head
And tension in my back
I hope we are on the right track
I hope by going back
And talking to my "child"
The anger that is wild
Can be made mild
Enough for me to face
And let joy take its place
As I go back in time and space
I see a place
Did you have one too?
A safe place for you
Ours was a tool shed
Except in our heads
It was a playhouse, a fort
A lean-to of sorts
Later we moved to a roof top
Because after that day we had to stop
Being in our safe place
And had to hide our face
When we wanted to explore
Our bodies anymore
I guess Mom had already called us
That's why we thought she made such a fuss
Of walking in on us
We knew we had no clothes on
But we were inside
Our own little house
Away from the World
When she saw us she whirled
And started to yell
And when that plastic belt fell
On our nakedness we knew

That we were through
The anger on her face
As she hit us every place
I'd never seen her like this
She didn't miss
I can feel the sting now
And I wonder how
Did her mom treat her this way?
Is this why we have to pay
For her fear
That brought the tears
Fear more than anger
I can still see her
I can't remember her words
Those I never really heard
Except that we were "bad"
And she would tell our dad
But the distorted look on her face
And the blows well placed
Make me know now
That she did not know how
To talk to us about us
Without making such a fuss
She could not explain it
She could only have a fit
The naturalness of it all
Our explorations she had to call
"Bad", because she had not been taught
She too, at sometime, had been caught
And punished severely
By someone she loved dearly
For exploring her brother
And probably another
Body like her own
Sometime before she was grown
How I've learned about sex mostly

Has been very costly
I've had to teach myself
From books off the shelf
And by lots of trial and error
Each time I remember the terror
That was not all I felt
As she applied that belt
She sent me on a trip of guilt
The return trip from guilt?
It's a slow trip back
Some day I may unpack
And find I have forgiven
And get on with livin'
Now that she is dead
I only have to get it straight in my head
That I am not so bad
But it really is sad
That we could not talk at all
When I was small
When I search in my head
For reasons for the anger and how it's fed
I find I have blocked out
Memories and feelings and doubts
When I was six, I could not go to school
Because of some rule
About my birth date
A rule I still hate
So when my mom and granny and aunt
Would get together to quilt
I would spend my time there
Under the frame and out of their hair
I made a "safe" place under there
The floor was my chair
My dolls and I would share
The threads and scraps
To make for them new wraps

Only when the ladies would leave to shop
They would leave me home with "Pop"
My Grandpop was quite old and kinda sad
I never thought of him as bad
And yet I guess I did
Because I had hid
The perverted reasons he sat me on his lap
While they were gone from home
His hands over my body would roam
When I'm much older I find
That these sessions did affect my mind
And how I feel about men
A lot of feelings were formed then
And today I sometimes still pay
With flashbacks in a way
Over which I have no control
They will still be there when I'm old
But now I can be bold
And face them and face me
And try to see
That it is all part of my past
It doesn't have to last
The anger that I feel
Even though it is very real
Doesn't have to be carried with me
I can be free
I can choose to lay it down
By sharing I have found
I'm not the only one who missed a lot of fun
When I was a kid
Because I hid
Behind my ignorance and fears
And frustrations and tears
My "child" is still present within
When will I begin
To choose to let my child out?

For me there is some doubt
But I know I'm ready to begin
Because I've looked within
And found I'm not so bad
In fact --- I'm good!

Fortieth Birthday

As I approach the fortieth
Anniversary of my birth
I have a tendency to look
Forward and reverse
To things I've done
Choices I've made
Games I've played
Masks I've worn
People I've known
Somehow they need to be examined now
For content and possible lessons learned
The regrets for things not tried
Seem to lessen as I try
More new things each day
The guilt, when recognized as such
Seems to be resolving
Some fears I've met head on
I'm able to face the dark now
And not shudder at the unknown
People who would have intimidated me at twenty
Amuse me now
Much of what I had feared
Has happened
And I have survived
To live again
Even fuller than before
'Though I have no idea
What's in store
The fear has been replaced by excitement
At the wonders of this World
The numbness I've felt

Intensifies my feelings
The pain I've felt
Is overridden now by joy
Having had my children
And loving them gives me a depth
I would not have had
'Though the absence of their presence
Causes such a void
The sensitivity I learned
While fulfilling their needs
Heightens my awareness
Of the needs of others
The ability to accept their childlike love
Freely given
Was something I needed to learn
For taking is as important as giving
And is much harder for me to do
My ability to share love
To open up myself
Is a growth I would never have believed
The ability to touch
To sense
To feel
To respond
To give
To reach out
To relieve
Myself and others through
The healing medium of love
I'm growing older
But I'm better too
There is less a need
To run away now
From the "me" I used to be
The "me" I am
Can now sit down and visit

With the "me" I can become
And in the time left which is mine
Hopefully we will resolve
The past and the future
Into a present of peace
Peace from the need to escape
Escape into shadows and numbness
No longer is my way
While escaping into shadows
I learned to fear the dark
Pills took me to a place in my brain
Where the negatives were insurmountable
Where hope was a lost art
It's a lie to pretend
That there are not still days
When I'd rather "numb out"
Than to face the pain
Of rejection
Of loneliness
Of grief
Of separation
In giving myself permission
To go back if the journey
Gets too tough
I also give myself
Permission to succeed or fail
My humanness was not acceptable
My weaknesses not allowed
The paradox comes in finding
My "weakness" to need love
Has become my greatest strength
The need to touch and be touched
Is no longer something I need to hide
Since I've quit judging myself so harshly
I can experience my life as a gift
Not fighting my impulses

Every step of the way
Permission to experience the good feelings
As well as the bad
Confronting change
I've found it is a friend
And the only constant factor in our World
Somehow within I have not given up
I will survive
I will find a way
A place to live the better life
The reflected life
With more meaning
More feeling
Than the drug-filled existence
Of the past
I cannot give up
I have come too far
Out of the darkness
To allow myself to sink
Back into oblivion
Just for security

Shopping

We run away to shop
You and I
My daughter
From their prying critical eyes
Their closed minds
We run to "togetherness"
To understanding
We run out to shop
Women have used it as an excuse
For years
For togetherness
For understanding
For time away
It's not so much the buying
As the sharing
Of time
Of ideas
Of feelings
Of needs
Of ourselves
Your grandmother and I
Did the same
And now you and I
We hold hands
We laugh
We analyze
The other shoppers
The fashions
The stores
Ourselves
Each other

Our family
And then we return
To "them"
Sometimes empty handed
Sometimes arms laden
We have shopped
And we are tired
But we are refreshed
Because we have shared

John

You came to me when I was wanting
Love, companionship, and children
And you fulfilled all three
But as the days passed we grew apart
And in my heart I knew
That through you I had grown and become
A person less fearful of myself
And had I known
What I know now
I might have explained it better
Maybe in a letter
That would have helped you understand
You were the man
I fell in love with
Because you're wonderful
And my leaving
Had less to do with you
Than me, I had to go
And try my wings and fly
And the other guy
Well, he helped me know me
And who I could be
If I set myself free
From my old restricted beliefs
And he fed my greed to understand all things
So you see
'Though I made you angry
And I upset the plan
Of perfect marriage, motherhood and man
We did survive, you and I
And I believe we're better

Because I dared to go
Don't believe I don't still grieve though
Now and then
Images of us together
As a family 'round the fire
Bring tears of love
Not extinguished
By the travel and the knowledge
And the lore
Why kill a love that served its purpose
That would be murder to grievous to bear
So when you think of me remember
In my heart I am your greatest fan
For you came to me when I needed
Companionship and children and love
And you let me go when I needed more...

Fear

The unknown
The known
The untrusted
Confusion
Expulsion of same
Our only resource
Confrontation
Obliteration by seeing
Knowing
No longer denying
The ultimate fear
Death
Terminal aloneness
Eons of time and space
And nothingness
Maybe there is
No God
No afterlife
Maybe this is all there is
Maybe this is not
All there is
Maybe we have
To answer to a deity
For all these acts
Done and undone
Thoughts expressed
And left unexpressed
The great paradox
Is death the end?
Do we get another chance?
And another

And another
Hence
The great fear...

Love

Love is letting go
Of fear
Love is accepting
Yourself
God
The Universe
Others
The Energy
From whence it all came
It all returns
To return again
And again
And again
And again
Until finally
We once again
Merge with
The Energy
The Divine Energy
Which is God
Until then
We are called
To practice
Love
Unconditional Love
Love that
Removes all fear

Forty-Fifth Birthday Reflection

Forty-five and feeling fine
Finding freedom in commitment
Commitment to self
To be the "me"
I contracted to be
Before I left the Source
To return to Earth
To search this plane for truth
Truth I find reflected
In rainbows
In clouds
Sunsets
Sunrises
Mountains
Seashores
And people
Yes, the people
They have the answer
And I know
That somewhere within me
So do I
This day I believe
The answer
Is Light
Light as Energy
Radiated through us
From the Source
To each other and back to the Source
Steiner calls it lemniscate
Jesus called it prayer
Some call it Reiki

I call it relief
It's a relief to know
It is not I who
Performs the miracles
But this "Force"
That works through me
An overall pattern for life?
At forty the question
Caused depression
At forty-five
It's relief
Because to search
And actually find it
Finally makes
So many things come clear
Reasons I chose
The paths I chose
Reasons I left
The paths I left
To search for new ones
Yet undefined
When the voices started
In my head
My mind filled with confusion
Until I took the time
To listen
To the rhythm
Of the words
And then their messages
Only to find
I had not lost
My mind but found it
And more that I had tapped
A frequency
Filled with beings
Working to help me see

The little "me"
Who felt sometimes scared
And alone
Could now feel protected
And nurtured
By the Higher Self
Which understood
The Universal Plan
For Humankind
The newness
Of the message
Was as old
As time itself
Humans know
The answers are within
And yet we've searched
Outside ourselves
For eons
For holy grails
And religions to pursue
And mountaintops in Tibet
For holy men
To tell us
"Man knows the answers
He must look within"
When we look within
We find fear
Anger
Deceit
Grief
Injustice
Lack of purpose
Scars of pains
Seemingly unrelated to our goal
And the message
But when we look in

And take them out
One by one
And retrace their cause
Or origination
We find
In terms of
The overall pattern
Of what we came to learn
They have their place
Their lesson
If you will
And we can let go
Forgive
And move on
At first it was
Like sorting
Through a trash heap
Sometimes like
Swimming in the sewer
But the more
Determined I became
To understand the pattern
The life purpose
And the more I could forgive
Both within myself
And others
I found
That peace was there
In the reclamation
That even the
Dung heap of incest
Has its purpose
And can be recycled
Into joy if we
Can live through it
As a lesson we've chosen

To learn to love
To love fully
Past the body
Past the mind
Into the soul
And beyond
To the Source
It's a lesson
In forgiveness
Of self
For it's all
The same Energy
And what one of us does
We all do
Or claim credit
Or blame
For the injustice
Or crime
Or glory
If you will
For the Energy
Knows no boundaries
Unless given those
By the brains of men
Truly it is infinite
And loving and kind
Through our thoughts
We have distorted
And forgotten
That we came
To love
To experience peace
And joy
Even though limited
Seemingly by these bodies
Our Spirits know better

And they are willing
To be released
When we've learned
The lessons we chose
Before we came
Once I believed
The name of the game
Of life was endurance
Now I know it's not
For I forgot
To see me
As I can be
And could only feel
The pain
The limitation
Which my negativity
Had caused
To limit my purpose
The pursuit
Of happiness
Instead of
Experiencing joy
No matter what I see
With my eyes
Or choose to feel
With my body
I now know
That behind
This illusion
The truth lay
And the truth
Is not a body
Or a belief
Or a place
Or a thing
For me

And of course
That's all I can see
Or say
Is the truth
For me today
Is life
In the quality
That I live it
The joy I'm willing
To experience
And pass on
That is truth
To it's fullest
To the max
So to speak
In the vernacular
Of youth
In this day
My children are
Still searching
But they seem
To have found
Their own answers
Which no longer
Lay in blaming me
For leaving them
To find me
We can rejoice now
That they are not my total reason for being
In this dimension
At this time
They know
There's more for me
And more for them
Than the limited existence
That we knew

Together
In Lubbock, Texas
In 1976

New Love

Trice I've known the death of love
In marriages to men too afraid to accept
Who they really were to share
Twice I've known the death of lovers
Yet I've lived to love again
I reason with myself
My love did not kill them
It helped them understand
The fullness of their lives on Earth
Now that I love yet again
I see - that as I experience me
There is a little fear there
From the past
That says, "Will this love last?"
Who knows and who cares?
A love not shared
Is a miracle lost

Remember

The Muse is out again
Filling pages with her ramblings
Your love has brought her voice, Dear,
Clearly to my mind
Now she wakes me at odd hours
With her music and her rhyme
She sends you love and greetings
Through the music of my mind
And stores the nurturing of memories
In words that come so clear
That you will hopefully remember
Why I hold you so very dear
I'm glad you're in my World
For without you it would not be complete
You've added a dimension
That would not have been
Had you not come to Earth to be my friend
I'm glad you're in my World
Each time we meet
There is something new
New words
New feelings
New actions
A new excitement
Born of not knowing
Who you are
Who I am
And yet I somehow feel
Even when we scratch the surface
And find ourselves in each other
The excitement will remain

We have journeyed far enough
From separate directions to this time and place
Having discovered our uniqueness
We are now not afraid to share
My words flow freely to you
And are given without fear
Of what tomorrow may bring
I grow weak from your touch
The look in your eyes
Is enough to make me flush
The sound of your voice
Causes me to smile
Your wanting me fills me
With a desire I had thought long dead
As I write to you
A warmth spreads through my thighs
Wishing you were here
To caress me in special places
With your gentleness
The touch of our love is tender
I cannot speak when you hold me
I become hopelessly lost in you
And lose the words to express my feelings
Quietly is how it begins
Learning to trust again
You are honest
You understand
We are surprising
Us, the walking wounded
With trails of tales
And slightly battered hearts
We are
Being mended by love
Together
We are special
Your love is special

I will hold it softly
And handle it with care
We came together not out of need but desire
A desire to love and be loved
A desire to cherish and be cherished
To fulfill to be filled full
Knowing that life is more than
Popcorn and movies
Walks in the woods
Champagne at midnight
Kites, balloons and sand castles
And bubble baths together
And chocolate kisses
And motorcycle rides
And making love all day
Or is it?
We came from that distant star
To enjoy the planet Earth
And each other
Remember?

Light Prisms

Laying with you in my arms
Watching light prisms dancing on the ceiling
Understanding the beauty
Of the clouds and trees
Making love till noon
In a myriad of ways
From tongue to toes
And back again
How lucky I am
To have a man who knows
The importance of my toes
And my brain
That purpose doesn't always mean intent
And desire's as beautiful
As completion
And builds more avenues for pleasure
Than any major city dares to boast
The thought of us together
Sparks desire within me
Rekindled by your coming
And you're going

Ah! Memories

Senses of pleasure
Found in exquisite places
Behind the ear
    The neck
    The down of hair
Between the thighs
That cry out for the touch
Of your hands
    Your tongue
    Your manhood
Sensual pleasure
    Candles
    Flowers
    Wine
    Fine food
    Beautiful music
    And you
'Midst laughter
    And sunshine
        And night
            And dreams........

    Ah! Memories....................................

Phantom Lover

He knew me when I didn't dare to speak
Of bodies and pleasure and loving
Before I knew that curves held more for me than geometry
He knew me before I knew that men
Were creatures to be comforted by kisses
He knew the frigid, fearful little girl
Who no longer comes to call
But his love prepared me for you
He took away the fear
That you might delight
In the newness of me
Who sings praises to your manhood
And my sensuality
So let's drink a toast
My Love, this night
"To my phantom lover"

Gods And Goddesses

Laying here beside you
Even after you've gone
I need no reassurance
Of your love
For you have left
A feeling deep within me
That I've not known before
I truly can be me
And you truly can be you
For we are gods and goddesses of love
And to nurture you
Nurtures me
And I see me in you
The male of me who understands
Computers and motors and time
And I'm encouraged
To find and explore
Parts of me I never knew before
Because you've come to share
Your reflection of me
For me to see
The beauty of you
Through me

The Dawn

Candles make shadows
On walls and ceilings
As our bodies turn
You moan your delight
As I stroke
Your manhood with my tongue
The silence interrupted only
By our cries
Of joy as you caress
My nest of love
My body shivers
And rivers of energy
Run from head to toe
And back again
Leaving me senseless
And drifting in space
With moonbeams
And shooting stars a plenty
Then the blissful dark
And you curled up beside me
As we wait for the dawn
To come again

Baby Birds

Outside my window
It's dawn
And fog rises
Ghostlike 'round the trees
In the stillness
I hear a baby bird
Nested on the window sill
His mother is gone
To find his breakfast
And he's not sure
She will return
I'm reminded of you
And our morning
On the porch
Watching baby birds
In first flight
So special
The times I've spent with you
At the beach
The kites, the crabs
The seagulls, the telephone booth
In the mountains
On your motorcycle
With me hanging on
For dear life
Except when I chose to wander off
On my own
Leaving only my body
There with you
While my consciousness
Soared on mountain tops

To explore
The meadows on the other side
We've had such fun
You and I
Remember?

How To Play

You teach me how to play, My Love
With bubbles and ducks and you
And clinging to your back
Around fast curves
And through long nights
Listening to music
Which makes no sense to me
Until you take it apart
Line by line
And horn by horn
And finally I understand
The meaning's
In the feelings
Not the notes or words
Life's such a pleasure
Such a joy
When we understand
That some days are made
For sleeping through
And making love
With slow passionate kisses
And showers
Cornflakes are out
And granola is in
With blueberries
So fresh the dew's still on
And real cream
And coffee
Rich with flavors
Furnished us by a friend
How well I remember

Those days with you
You taught me how to play again
When I had all but forgotten
The little girl inside of me
Who cries out to be free
From restrictions
Of "shoulds" and "should not's"
Of "oughts" and "ought not's"
You handle her so well
She loves the little boy in you
As well as the man
Who's gentle enough
To understand
It takes a while
To relearn
How to play
When you've been
"Grown up" all your life

Little Robert

Remember little Robert? I do
And what you told me is true
You said he would one day be free
To come out and play with me
You said, "He will come unafraid"
And willing to trade
His feelings and his love
And together you can rise above
The conventions of this World
He will teach you games
Without boards or words or names
With him you will relearn play
You need not be careful what you say
He will accept you as you are
Because he too has come far
He will not laugh when you cry
But will always try
To understand your pain or grief
Accepting tears as your relief
He will not expect more than you have to give
Your love will help him live
Your caring will provide a way
To help him make it thru the day
When the hours are long
And things may seem wrong
Offering yourself will truly be enough
To warrant being loved

To Dream

Did you ever take a train?
I didn't
But I know what it's like
It's like being carried
Over hills and valleys
In the belly of a snake
But there are windows
To look out
And someone else drives
And you can sleep
Or read
Or dream
I've never ridden on a train
But I know how it feels to dream

Loving You

You nurture me in ways
You may not understand
The joy of you, as you are
The you, you strive to be
The money that you send
To meet my daily needs
You, My Friend, are special
And if you really knew
You'd be more satisfied
With you

The Simple Life?

Music and spices
And diamonds and jewels
Were things of kings and queens
In days of yore
Today its cars and boats
And stocks and notes
And places in the sun
And proper schooling
For the kids
And orthodontists
For their teeth
And skiing and dancing
And lessons of every sort
What happened to the simple life
And you and I and time to spend
Examining the grass for shamrocks
And seeing pictures in the clouds
Want to take a walk?

David

Austin's city limits
Brings the lights of remembering
You as teacher
Me as student
Your towering masculine frame
Your self assurance
Intrigued me
Enough to drop my reserve
To reach out to you
As woman
When you "accepted"
Nay "rejoiced"
At my boldness
A magic came to life
I needed strength
Humor, reassurance
Understanding and love
Your needs were the same
The gentleness of you
Wrapped in such strength
Was frightening to me
You were
A new phenomenon
For me
A man with feelings
Willing to express
In words if not emotion
Confounded me
And my stereotypes
Of what policemen are
And would be

We shared the magic
Of caring
And words
The poetry, music
Flowers and wine
And physical closeness
We were wonderful
Until I could
Not resist
Projecting us into
The future
And in the image
I was lost
I ran, you moved
But we left a trail of letters
We did not need
Sherlock Holmes to follow
Periodically when we
Came together again
And shared our magic
We knew
We would always
Be there
For each other
No matter who else
Came into our lives
For we are committed
At a level
That makes resistance
A lie
Friendship of this nature
Leaves passion
In the shade
Intercourses of words
Feelings, emotions, caring
Not found

Anywhere else
When I left again
You wished
Me well "God's speed"
You mentioned too
"I have a friend"
"I want to share"
"With you"
I never dreamed in this ultimate act
Of unconditional love
All you were giving
You and me and him
But you're in "our" home
In Denver this night
And Austin welcomes me
To yours
This ultimate
Triangle of love
No matter how often
It is squared by the presence
Of another woman
Has brought me
More love and peace
And sharing than most women
Ever dream
And I am
Eternally grateful
For you, My Friend
And the magic we share

Jealousy

It's 4:00 a.m.
And I've awakened
Missing you
You said you'd call
And it's not like you
Not to do the things you say
How are you?
I know it's not easy
To watch your worldly goods
Being boxed away
And swallowed up
By an impersonal
Trailer truck
Where did you sleep?
I didn't get a chance to ask you
Where you'd be
Until you come to me
Next week
Right now you feel
So far away
Yet you're right here
Beside me in my mind
I'm glad you got to ride today
'Though I wish
It had been with me
Trading the Cascades
For the Rockies
And leaving old friends
That's got to be hard
I've spent the day
Burning more of the past

Old cards, old letters and photos
How can anything
That feels so good
Hurt so bad?
Every letting go is
A step forward
So "they" say
Let's hope "they" know
What's good for us
'Cause it hurts like hell
To give up the past
When the future's
Dimly lit and changing
All the while
My chart says of today
"You'll be torn between two worlds"
How true
I wish I had
Come with you
To say goodbye
To the beautiful skies
Of Oregon
And to the trees
And God, those mountains!
But I choose to write
How dumb I feel!
Missing you like this
I never meant to love you
Only share our bodies
For awhile
And maybe some good ideas
You know?
I never mean to love you
Or care
If you're in some other
Woman's arms

I never meant to love you
But I do
So hurry home to Denver
'Cause someone's missing you
Sounds like
Another hokey
Country and western tune
Can you believe it?
This must be
How that stuff
Gets written
Not being able to sleep
And falling in love
And letting the emotions out
Pretty scary stuff, I'd say
Rambling on this way
When I should be sleeping
And not missing you
But I do
And I'm not sorry
Except for the jealousy
That's a sin
For me
'Cause it's not loving
Unconditionally
And I want to
But it's hard
To think of someone else
Holding you
When I want to
Even if she's just your friend
And she knows about me
Your phone rang
To an empty house tonight
Because I'm missing you
Hurry home, My Love

To a warm bed
And gentle kisses
And arms that miss you

Cherished

At night
When the lights go out
I curve myself
To match your back
Listen to your breathing
Feel your warmth
Your muscles relax
Later, when I turn over
You curve yourself
To match my back
I feel cherished…

When you arise
Before I do
And you adjust
The covers against my back
As you leave the bed
I feel cherished…
Sometimes
Without warning
You take my hand
And bring my fingers
To your lips
I feel cherished…

Sometimes
I reach out
And touch
Your forehead
Your temple
The back of your neck

For no reason
Except to let you know
I cherish you...

Corporate

Daily
You play a game, My Love
In the corporate arena
Of life
The sense of
Corporate purpose
Power, money
The sense of your
Personal purpose
Love
Healing
Cooperation
Dedication to ethics
Ideals
Philosophical theories
Reiterated through
Emotionally scarred
Vehicles of expression
Who fear losing
Their rung
On the corporate
Ladder to success
Overshadow logic
Reason and sanity
With intimidation
Confusion
Using
Reducing
Instead of building
Healing
God-Light

Cosmic Vision
Universal purpose
Unable to reduce itself
To the pettiness
Of egos
And tirades
Will prevail
The question
We all ask
My Love
Is
When?

True Desires

Men and women
Seeking to be cherished
Understood and loved
Begin cycles of searching
For partners in crimes
To disillusionment
We pretend to look
But not seek
For a body, a heart
In which to entrust
Our soul's desire
Acceptance
We barter with sex
Money, dreams and schemes
For illusive security
And call it love
We find tramping
Through our hearts and minds
Parades of people
Disillusioned by sameness
And promises and pain
Seeking love
Finding fear of being
Found wanting
Acceptance and love
Because it's hard to admit
Our true desires
To strangers and ourselves

Emotions In Reserve

You touched me in places of allowing
That had not been touched before
I did not have to give up me
To be loved by you
You saw my potential
Nurtured it
Inspired it to grow
Beyond my bounds of knowing
Reasons were not always given
Nor expected
My physical pleasure
Did not compete or preclude your own
But they were interdependent
For you gained from my joy
Experienced through our touch
Just as much as I
You knew no bounds
In loving me extravagantly
        decadently
        sensuously
Yet you held back
A part of you in reserve
Emotions
Not to be known
Trusted, understood or shared
You were willing to share our pleasure, not pain
Identity hidden by compassion
Rejoicing in the moment
Past and future exempt
From tarnish of emotion
You soared inside yourself

And cried there too
Hidden from view or trust
You felt in secret
Emotions rampant held in check
So anger, rage, discontent
Could not spill over into reality
And mar illusion

Borders

Borders vanish
When bodies touch
In passion
Illusion reigns
And pain of loneliness
Subsides as passion rises
Bodies touch
Souls employ
Reason to understand
Thoughts, expressions
Feelings are
Beauty is
No explanation necessary
Desire sees reason
As an adversary
Guilt an enemy
Of copulation's beauty
Friendship finds boundaries
To identify, restrain
Its goal a mockery
Of passion
Senselessness
Encounters grief
When friendship
Cannot survive passion
Borders appear

Truth Hides In Anger

Truth is seldom heard
When hearts are wounded
Feelings send truth hiding
Behind remarks designed
To inflict pain.
Compassion honors truth
Within the recesses of its knowing
Understanding the morrow will bring
Regret for "truth" spoken in anger.
Erasure, retraction imperative
'Though impossible
When feelings subside
And truth again has its day
The damage is done.
Scars born of anger, resentment last longer
Than scars of accidents or play
Broken bones mend quicker
Than broken hearts.

Trading Places

To see my view
Would require
That I move
And let you be
In my place
I may not know
Your view
But I can have
A healthy respect
For how you acquired it
'Though it seems
Foreign to me
And mostly dense
For I see through
A fog of suspicion
And greed
And a need to please
And you see through
Your need
And desire
To be understood
But not exposed
For expectations
Of understanding
Are only born
Of trust

Similarities vs Differences

When we met
We saw what we wanted
To see similarities
Ourselves in each other
Reflected in a new way
A way that looked
And felt alive, reborn
Enchanted by romance
We grew
To see illusion
Give way to a desire
To be known
For whom we really are
And to be accepted
Some of the magic went
When illusion
Gave way to routine
And sameness
We identified differences then
Forgot similarities
Enchantment
Romance
Magic
And never made it
To whom we really are
Or acceptance

Questioning

You've told me you love me
You've said it so many times
In so many ways
That I've grown to believe you mean it
'Though I wonder still
Why me - when I leave so much of me
Behind when I'm with you
You know only the parts of me I can safely share
There is so much I have to give, to share
That I've hidden inside
Buried beneath doubt
And shame and fear
And I so want to bring it out
And shout "love all of me or none"
For the game is up
I've lied by saying only half truths
To spare you pain
For there is nothing to gain
In risking your wrath or sadness
By sharing my doubts and fears
Will there ever be one who will come
To share it all
The pain
The joy
The laughter
And the doubts
I wonder
"Does such a one exist?"

Brown-Eyed Man

The brown-eyed man is back
Is he a dream?
An illusion
Or a hope
Or is he real
An aspect of me unrealized
Sought, but found only in illusive glimpse
As a day dream
Where are you, my friend?
Why do you hide?
Inside of me, or out?
Why can I not have you here now?
To hold
Illusive whisperings of love
Coming through times tunnel of thought
Bring me words of love
I wish to hear
The reddish golden hue
Of the hair on your chest
Soft under the gentle
Caress of my finger tips
So real it takes my breath away
And yet - is it a mere imagining?
Or do you really exist
Somewhere out there
Gaining glimpses of me
And wondering for your sanity?
I pledge myself to know
The truth of you
I ask the illusion to become real
That you walk into my life

And prove to me
God exists in man
A man not afraid to love me
Without the need to change me
Rearrange me
Or keep me in a cage
If you exist
I call you forth
My illusive brown-eyed man

Love or Loneliness

When I hear you're ill
Shudder goes thru my form
Can it be born of love or loneliness?
For times we shared
As husband and wife
Do I still care so much
That when I think of you now
The tears that fill my eyes are hot
Held back only through sheer intention
I do not fully understand
These reactions I feel today
The body rages to be held
Caressed, kissed and loved
As I enumerate the men I've shared
Looking for a past to relive
Rather than to start an unknown future
With someone new
I can't find a soul, still living
I can go to today and say
"Hold me, say kind words, let me know you care"
Without starting a renewal of repercussions
I can not afford
But as I think back to each one
I see a pattern formed of fear to share my all
With any one of them
If they only knew
The depths of me
Could they review it all
And call me sane
And remain to learn about
The parts of me I still doubt

Or would they run
From the fun of knowing
Of sharing it all
I can't recall a soul
Who's shared it all
Maybe no one really wants to know it all
Can we ever become so aware
That we can share
And compare
Our pain and sorrow and joy
And not employ the guilt
Of our ancestors and our families
To win the battle over illusion
I've done enough
To confuse my brain
Only something's still remain
Unresolved like riddles
Thinking back through relationships
And delusion and pain
I wonder what I would gain
If I claimed my freedom to be
Who and what I really am
To please me and not a man?

Threads Of Life

There's a bigger picture here
And more people are involved
Than you and I
We are only
A few interwoven threads
In a larger tapestry
And there are mysteries
I don't try
To understand them all
Part of the fun
Is standing in awe
We don't have to understand
The Ocean - to swim in it
We can be instruments
And cheerleaders
For our souls
Without fully having
To understand

Student - Teacher

When the student is ready
The teacher appears
Everywhere
In the sky
In the trees
In taxi cabs
And banks
In therapists' offices
Service stations
In our friends
In our enemies
We're all teachers
We're all students
Everything is an oracle
Clouds, cats, the sky
Rain and lightening
Gaze into a stone
Listen to the rain
Understand
The hidden secrets
Of the Universe
It's all connected
Every piece mirrors
The whole
When you have
Eyes to see
And ears to hear

Ah Ha!

Something was
Troubling me
Like I was
Missing something important
Like a word
Or a name
Which I couldn't remember
But was on the tip of my tongue
I looked down to see
A Gecko run across
The bare wooden floor
I also saw my feet
And it dawned on me
Where ever I go
I am there
The answer
Is not
In one place
But in all places
Inside of me

True Teachers

True teachers
Create lives
Which create
Bridges of example
Over which
They invite
Their students
To cross
Having facilitated
Their crossing
They encourage
Students
To create
Bridges and lives
Of their own
For other students
To cross
To create
Bridges

With Great Love

Accept everything
Do what you can
Flow with the rest
We cannot always
Do great things in life
But we can do
Small things with great love...
Kind words
Can be short
And easy to speak
But their echoes
Are endless...

True Friendship

I was hungry
And you fed me
I was thirsty
And you gave me water
I was a stranger
And you welcomed me
Naked
And you clothed me
Ill and you
Comforted me
I became strong
And you loved me
Still

Love

There is no way to peace
Peace is the way...
There is no way to happiness
Happiness is the way...
There is no way to Love
Love is the way...

Love
Understand
Trust
The wisdom of the Universe
Do what you can
Then let go
And only love...

Inner Travel

When you learn
Inner travel
Your consciousness
Will never again
Be limited by space
Or time
Or the confines
Of the physical body
Imagination
Is the first step
The bridge
To clairvoyant sight

The Way Home

Consciousness refracts
Through the prism
Of the soul
To become
Three forms of light
Three selves
The Ego Self
Cares for
And protects
The physical body
The Conscious Self
Guides
Informs
Interprets for
And reassures
The Ego Self
The Higher Self
Radiates love
Reminding
Inspiring and
Rekindling
The sparks of light
Within the Conscious Self
Eternally patient
And understanding
It waits
To join
The other two
To synergistically
Form a whole
Greater than

The sum of its parts
To bring
Them all home
To GOD

No Maps

There are no maps
No creeds
No philosophies
To lead us home
The directions come
Straight from the UNIVERSE

No Duality

With eyes
That see no duality
But the invisible World
The larger view of life
No "me" and "others"
No separate self
No light, no shadow
Nothing within
Or without
Not made
Of Spirit
Then and only then
Will our Spirits carry us--Home to the Light

Just...

To be is to do
To do is to be
Do-be-do-be-do
Just do...
Just be...

Thoughts - Ideas

Thoughts and ideas
Are like tiny seeds of life
In the Universe
Each has the ability
To set in motion
Acts
That range in effect
From below measure
To monumental...

Limited knowledge
Doing its best
Out shines
Superior knowledge
Sitting at rest...

Joy For A Rainy Day

I want to find the space
Within me
Where I stored joy
For future days
And unleash it...

No Death

Do not stand
At my grave and weep
I am not there
I do not sleep...

I am in every wind that blows
I am in the sparkle
On new fallen snow
I am in sun light
Reflections on the lake
I am still here to give
And not to take
I am in the gentle rain
Trickling down
Your window pane...

Do not stand
At my grave
And cry
I am not there
My spirit
Did not die...

Life And Art

I discovered
What I knew
Was also what matters

Integrity
Idealism
Beauty
Grace
Charm
Romance
Passion

I chose not to
Go home again
To fall once again
From the phony grace
Of good intentions
And elevated expectations

I chose instead
To live
To be me
I found
Being myself
Was an acquired taste
At first salty
With tears
And bitter
With memories
But later
Sweet with joy

And expectations of good...
As my motive shifted
From seeking happiness
To creating it...

The equation
Between life and art
Has not proven to be simple
Because I have only
Language and feelings
To share my journey
My soul hands out the tickets
A most ghostly kind of travel

I learn to keep the lessons
As I learn them
And throw away the experiences
To make more room for joy...

Swinging The Pendulum Between Solitude And Communion

In retreat
I learn things
  To carry back
    To daily life...

Sea Shells

Why do shells
Fascinate me so
Their beauty
Their shapes
Their intricacies
Their textures
Their designs
Spirals
Winding inward
Or is it that they
Were once homes
Shelters
For vulnerable creatures
Such as I
I collect them
Hold them
Admire them
Search for them
And their uniqueness
Endlessly
On seashores
From coast
To coast
And beyond
There is
A memory
There for me
Vague
But haunting
Of my life
Before Earth
And my home
Shells remind me…

Islands

We are all islands
In a common sea
We are
In the last analysis
Alone
And yet never alone...

In Kauai

What a relief
To write or paint
So that one
Forgets one's companion
Forgets where one is
Or what one is
Going to do next
To be drenched in work
After one has been drenched
In sleep
Pencils, pads
Paper and paints
Creative disarray
We are swept clean of duties
And demands of the outside World
Reeling a little we return
From our intense absorption
We return with relief
To small chores
Of getting lunch
As if eating
Were our lifeline
To reality
We welcome the firm ground
Of physical action
Under our feet
As we take a brief walk
As we have almost drowned
In the sea of emotional
And intellectual work
Our souls seek

To be expanded
Building within us
A thirst for knowledge
For magnitude
For Universality
For immensity
For interstellar space

Island Life

Island life
Oddly enough
Gives us a limitless feeling
A pattern of freedom
Within which to create
An easy unforced rhythm occurs
A natural balance
Of physical
Intellectual
And social life
A space within which
To create works
Not deformed by pressures
Of the outside World

The Pendulum Swings

I pack to leave the island
And ask myself
What do I have to show
For my time here?
For my ruminations
A few paintings
A few pages of writing
A few answers
No real solutions
Maybe a few clues
Only a few
Of how to proceed
A decision made
Clutter must go
Excess and trivia
Restrict, distract, and fragment me
Space is needed
With a few perfect specimens
Surrounded by space
It is in space
That beauty breathes and blooms
Space allows
For uniqueness
Significance
Expansion
Growth
Oriental artists
Understand space
Simplicity
Selectivity
Less is more

Space holds infinite possibility
The multiplicity of the World
Crowds in on me
With its false sense of values
Values weighed in quantity
Not quality
In speed, not stillness
In noise, not silence
In words, not thoughts
In acquisition, not beauty
I need solitude
And space
To nourish me
I seek simplicity of living
As much as possible
To retain true awareness
Of life, of beauty
To work without pressure
To balance
Physical, intellectual, spiritual life
Space for significance, beauty, truth
Time for sharing
And solitude
Closeness to nature
To truly understand
And accept its cycles
The intermittency of life
Human relationships
The Spirit
I desire to live
A reflective life
A creative life

Daydreaming

Daydreaming
Demands something
Of us
Unlike TV
Or the movies
Books
Music
Or the radio
In daydreaming
In solitude
We let things
Occur to us
We can hear
Our own
Inner music
From inside
And beyond

A Stranger To One's Self

When one is
A stranger to one's self
One's self is
Estranged from
Others
When one
Is out of touch
With one's self
One cannot
Touch others
When we
Meet ourselves
Become acquainted
Know ourselves
We meet
No strangers
We can touch
And be touched

Woman's Creation Invisible

Except for her children
Woman's creation
Is oft' invisible

We All Have A Need

We all have a need
For purpose
To feel indispensable
We feel hungry
Not knowing
What we hunger for
We fill the void
With food
And distractions
We hunger
For purpose
To fulfill
To feel filled full

Claiming Solitude

Claiming creative solitude
A reasonable ambition
Takes inner conviction
To create
Difficult to
Tell friends
And family
I cannot come
This is "my" day
"My" hour
To be alone
In our society
When one shows
The need
To be alone
One is considered
Strange
Suspect
One must make apologies
Make excuses
Hide the fact
That they practice
Solitude

How To Feed The Soul

Aware of our hunger
Our needs
We are
Unaware
Of how
To feed ourselves
Our souls
Ignorant
Of what will satisfy
Our longing
Quiet time alone
Contemplation
Prayer
Music
A centering
Line of thought
Or reading
Study
Creative expression
Physical
Or intellectual
Any creation
Proceeding
From within
Arranging flowers
Writing a poem
To be
Inwardly attentive
Feeds the soul
Inwardly directed
We find

Inner strength
Inner solutions
For outward living

We Have

We have the desire to be
Accepted as whole
To be seen
As individuals
To give ourselves
Completely
And with purpose

The "Old Paradigm" Of A New Relationship

How beautiful
Is fist meeting
Two people
With no history
As yet co-created
Between them
Newness
Excitement
Listening intently
Feeling intently
No others involved
Perfect unity
In an instant
Free of ties
Chains
Complications
Expectations
Responsibilities
No worry about
The future
Or debts
To the past
How swiftly
How inevitably
The perfect unity
Is invaded
The relationship changes
Becomes complicated
By its contact
With the World
Pure relationship

Is limited
In space
And in time
Its essence
Implies exclusion
It excludes
The rest of life
Other relationships
Other sides
Of personalities
Other responsibilities
Other possibilities
Of futures
It excludes
Growth
There is no holding
Of a relationship
To a single form
This is not tragedy
But part of
The miracle
Of life and growth
Duration
Is not a test
Of true or false
Validity has no
Relation to time
To duration
To continuity

The "New Paradigm" Of A New Relationship

The new relationship
Of two whole people
Meeting and touching
Dancing
With space
So the winds of Heaven
May dance between them
A relation of persons
As persons
Their values
Within themselves
Two solitudes protected
Choosing to meet
To greet
To share
To touch
A moreHuman love
A love more divine
A love of evolution
Unfolding
Not a result
Of accident
But of achievement
Development
Of self
Maturation
Of Spirit
Of understanding
Through
Relating to self
A creative love

Not creating other bodies
But more love
Two solitudes
Who have become
Worlds in themselves
Can now live
Side by side
Accepting
That even between
The closest human beings
Infinite distances
Exist
They can love
And succeed
At love
If they can
Love the distance
Between them
Which makes
It possible
To breathe
To see the sky
And the other
In their wholeness
And beauty

Pioneers Of Togetherness

We are pioneers
Seeking a path
Through the maze
Of tradition
Convention
Dogma
Theory precedes exploration
Our efforts
A struggle
To mature
The concept
Of male/female
Relationships
Every step
Even a tenative one
Has value
Every advance
In understanding
Counts
During
These experiences
We glimpse
An essence illustrated
What the new relationships
Might become
One perfect day
Can give us clues
Of a more perfect life
Any good relationship
Illuminates
All relationships

A Good Relationship

A good relationship
Has a pattern
Like a dance
Built on the
Same rules
Dancing partners
Do not need
To hold on tightly
Because they
Move confidently
In the same pattern
Accepting
Improvisation
As a creative challenge
No place for
The possessive clutch
The clinging arm
No heavy hand
To break the rythym
Only the barest touch
In passing
Now arm and arm
Now face to face
Now back to back
It does not
Matter which
Because they know
They are partners
Moving to the same rhythm
Creating a pattern together
And allowing themselves

To be invisibly nourished
By the relationship
Not strangled
By claims
Intimacy
Tempered by lightness
Of touch
Allows endless change
Beauty of unfoldment
The joy of living
In creation
In participation
In the moment

One can only dance well
In the beat of the moment's music
One can only relate well
In the moment
Why is it so difficult?

It is fear
Which makes us clutch
Fear destroys
The winged life
Fear can only be exorcized
By its opposite
Love

The Pendulum Swings Between Sharing And Solitude

It is the swinging of
The pendulum between
The opposite poles
Of sharing and solitude
That makes a relationship nourishing
To share profound thought
And then to touch
The swing between sharing and solitude
To be able to swing
From the intimate
The particulars
The functional
Out into the abstract
The universal
And then back to the personal again
The meeting of two solitudes
As it was meant to be

When I Love

When I love someone
I do not love them
All the time
In the same way
From moment to moment
It is impossible
It would be a lie to pretend
It is so
Many demand this
They have so little faith
In the ebb and flow
Of life, of love, of relationships
Insistence
On permanency
On duration
On continuity
When the only continuity possible
In life as in love
Is growth
In fluidity
In freedom
Security in relationship
Lies not in looking back
Nor forward with dread or anticipation
But in being fully present
Accepting love
And the other
For what it
And they are now

A Mid-Life Crisis

A mid-life crisis
Can be a time
To escape
  Into depressions
  Nervous breakdowns
  Drink
  Love affairs
  Or frantic
    thoughtless
    fruitless
    work
Or a time
Of shedding
Shells
Masks
False ambitions
Material accumulations
Possessions
Ego
Pride
Armor
Competitive drive
For what?
To find one's self
To practice
The art
Of inward looking
To claim
Autonomy
Creativity
Adventure

Lust for life
Just for the living
Romance
Simplicity
Exploring
Intellectual
Cultural
Spiritual activities
Or daydreaming
To be pursue
At leisure
Time to pursue
The neglected side
Of one's self
Free for growth
Of mind
Heart
Talent
And soul

The Astronaut's View Of Earth Changed Us

Today a planetary point of view
Has burst upon Humankind
With the View of Earth
From beyond
Captured on film
The Earth is rumbling
And erupting
In ever widening circles around us
The tensions, conflicts, sufferings
Even in remote areas touch us
Via satellites
We cannot avoid these vibrations
The inter-relatedness
Of the World
Links us with more people
Than our hearts can hold
Our Minds, our imaginations
However are infinite
And can contain it all
We cannot act upon it all
As we are want to do
As we were taught to rescue
Because we have extended our circle
Throughout space and time
How can we adjust?
Our Puritan consciousness
To Planetary awareness
We talk about the problems
Out there in the World
Because we feel so inadequate
To solve our own

We cannot positively effect
The periphery of the circle
Unless we work from the Center
When we start at the Center of ourselves
We discover something worthwhile
Extending toward the periphery
Of the circle...

Be Here Now

The individual is dwarfed
By the enormity of the mass
The present is overlooked
In our insatiable appetite for the future
We never appreciate the here and now
Until it is challenged
When the future becomes perilous
The good past is far away
The near past is painful
The present has a chance
To expand into an eternity
Of a golden here and now
In which we can enjoy
The vividness of here
The spontaneity of now...

New Consciousness

A new consciousness
Is creeping across the old
Engulfing it
As an antibiotic wiping out a dread disease
Of limitation
Stagnation
Expansion of consciousness
To include all races, all sexes
Liberation to face
A changing World
With new awareness of problems created
By the changes
Problems which cannot be solved
By men, by women, alone
But can only be surmounted
By men and women
Side by side...

New Communications

Male/female communications
Moves from fighting/sulking
To confrontation with love
No longer saying
If you don't understand
I can't possibly tell you
Changing to
I'm not sure...
But it feels like...
Yes, I think I see
It may be similar to
When I feel...
Holding open space
In which to examine
Possibilities for hearing
For being heard
With doors left ajar
In minds once closed
By expectations and societies
Defined roles
Of men and women
Seek to open wide
Doors left ajar
In minds willing
To truly communicate
Daring to hear
Daring to be heard...

The Unknown

It is the unknown
With all its disappointments
And surprises
That is most enriching
And exciting

Relationships That Work

What does it take
To create a relationship
That works?

Love, caring, kindness
Differences enough
To make conversation
That doesn't bore

Belief in self and others
As capable and deserving of love
When we desire the same, or similar
Structure or goals, we have a chance
Of success, not at romance
But at love and relationship

To have a relationship
By the word itself implies
Relating
Not just, "What happened to you today?"
But "How did it make you feel?"

The boss' words
The color of the clouds
The "will work for food" sign
In the hands of the man on the corner
The rainbow after the shower

What do you think?
How do you feel?
What do you desire?

Sharing these things without fear
That's what causes a relationship to last
But, of course, good sex helps ☺

The Rain

The rain falls
When we least expect it
To wash away
Our tears

The snow falls
Forming a blanket of white
To cover the ugliness
Of winter's blight

But nothing covers the pain
Not rain
Nor snow
But time

Time alone erodes
The fissures pain has wrought
We see the change
Before we feel relief

The first sunshine
After the rain
Forms a rainbow
Reminding us...

Of hope...

Soul Music

The notes of music
Mean nothing to me
A G B D F
DO RE ME FA SO LA TE DO
But in my heart
Mind, body and soul
I hear songs
And melodies
Which sound foreign
To that which
I hear
Here on Earth
The resonance
Within
Clears me
And brings me joy
I cannot make
It appear
But when I
Write, paint
Walk in the forest
Or make love to you
It flows
Without ceasing
As a cosmic
Serenade
To our love

Love Doubt

Do not doubt
I love you
Because I'm
Not beside you
Always
Physically
If you do
You do not
Understand
The nature
Of my love
For when
I love
I hold the object
Of my love
Within a sacred space
Inside my being
Where I nurture it
Cultivate it
Protect it
Pray for it
Love it
So that when
I return to you
There is more
Of me
And more of you
For us to love

Intention

Your physical form
So much larger
Than mine
And yet
When you
Embrace me
I do not feel
Overshadowed
Or fearful
I feel protected
Equal
And somehow
More whole
Your intention
Effects my feelings

Holy Communion

Our multi-dimensional selves
Met in Holy Communion
Their discussions
And decisions
Brought our meeting
Forth
That we might live out
An example
Male/female love
Whole
Independent
Interdependent
Interwoven
But not enmeshed
In personality's clutter
So synergy
Can take place
To affect
The whole
Of Humankind
Calling a truce
Creating a well
Filled with
Balanced energy
Of love
Of hope
From which
Others can draw
To end the war
Between the sexes

Hands That Serve

Business and trollies
And dollies and toys
And boys and rainbows
And frogs and leaps
And tea that steeps
On kitchen stoves
Well worn with love's abundance
Shown through hands that serve
The master of each soul

Through The Eyes Of A Child

Kites and rainbows
And simple things
Cultivated to employ
The mind of senselessness
For reasons of joy
To nourish the spirit
The soul divine
The music of Angels
And children
And wind
And rain
For kites and rainbows
To nourish the soul
Circuses and rainbows
And kites and kings
These are the things
That make us want
To be kids again
For to see through the eyes
Of the child, you see
Is the age old admonition
Of our Lord
The World is to enjoy

Oh, Sweet Soul Of Mind

Oh, sweet soul of mine
Which understands
That pain from love and scars of past
Needn't last
That today's truth
Oft' becomes
Tomorrow's lie
And today's lies oft' become
Tomorrow's truths
Because life changes
And evolves
And if I evolve
To understand
That I'm the maker
Of my truth
Of my past and
Of my destiny
Then only then
Oh, sweet soul of mine
Will I know and understand
What I came to Earth to learn

Illusion Of Death

For every life there is a plan
Set out by God and man
Before he comes to this good Earth
To experience restriction
In physical form
To prove to himself he can remember
Where he really is inside
Before and after all else
There is no death
Illusion's greatest joke
Perpetuated by man
To scare himself
Into believing
He is separate
From God

Earth

Mother Earth is crying
Her sobbing
Comes as earthquakes
To the cities of the World
Her tears flow
Lavalike
From volcanic ducts
The acid rain
Of thoughtlessness
Kills her vegetation
And her streams
What happened to her dream?
Of Eden
And man and woman sharing
Life in a garden
Of beauty and love
It's coming
But first the rain
Of remembering
Must fall
Into every heart
To wake the "being" there
Who understands
Mother Earth is us
And we are she

Trials Of Life On Earth

Such are the trials of life on Earth
The mortgages and insurance
The time tables and time clocks
The uncertainty – not knowing
If the paycheck will stretch
To cover one more installment
And about that water leak
But Oh!The joy of it!
The sky, the wind, the trees
The birds, the clouds, the people
Yes, the people – they really
Make this trip worthwhile.

Spirals Of Energy

Quantum leaps
Millennium conversions
Spirals of energy
Complete within man
Mother Nature's plan is served
By denizens of the deep
As well as those who sleep for centuries
Before returning to complete
A mission left wanting
In some previous time
Through quantum leaps
Millennium conversions
And spirals of energy
It is done

Evolution

Evolution of man
Survival of the fittest
New age challenges
Beyond war
To universal peace
Seeing Earth as an ally
A ship that we ride
Through time and space
Giving loving maintenance
To our vessel, Terra
It is time

Time

Time is illusive
Some days are packed
With hours unfulfilled
Others have minutes
Drawn out forever
Until I think
I'll scream before the day is through
Time created by man
To try to understand
And give perspective
To the Third dimension
Of Earth
And his activities here
A way to count
And sequence
Events
But we've learned
That other dimensions
Do not recognize
The restriction of time
And to limit ourselves
To the now
And not understand
That we are in control still
Of our pasts
And our future
That they are all
The now
Really is a disservice
Even to time

Reason

Seasons and reasons
And scores of other things
Deliberately confuse us
From the meaning of it all
Life is here for the living
Life's to be a ball
With costumes and magic
And incense and love
The theatre of the mind
Creating images and caricatures
Illusions of a sort
Which further Nature's plan
And give reason to man

Transformation

A moment comes
When there is a shift
From destruction of the old
To birthing of the new
The crisis is over
The process is poetic
It is like
A butterfly emerging from a cocoon
Coming out of a dark cave
Into a lovely day
Shedding skins of old
Ways, old pain, beliefs, ideas, attitudes, ways
Breathing deeply of freshened air
Being born again
For a new time
An incredible tomorrow